Live with meaning. Die with passion.

Fumitada Naoe
CEO of Sanctuary Corporation, a funeral service company

One Peace Books, inc.

Contents

Live with meaning. Die with passion.

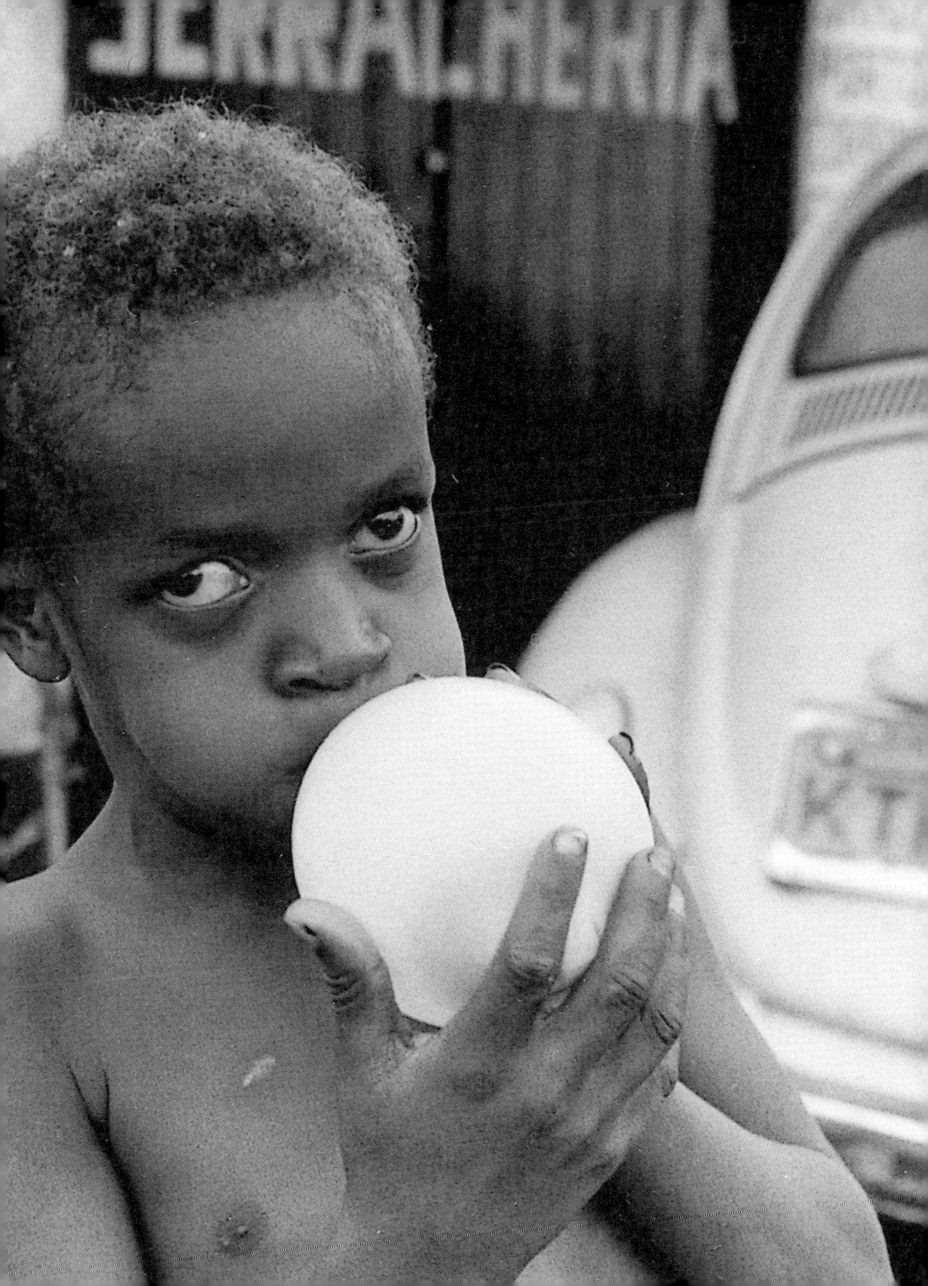

CHAPTER 1

LIFE

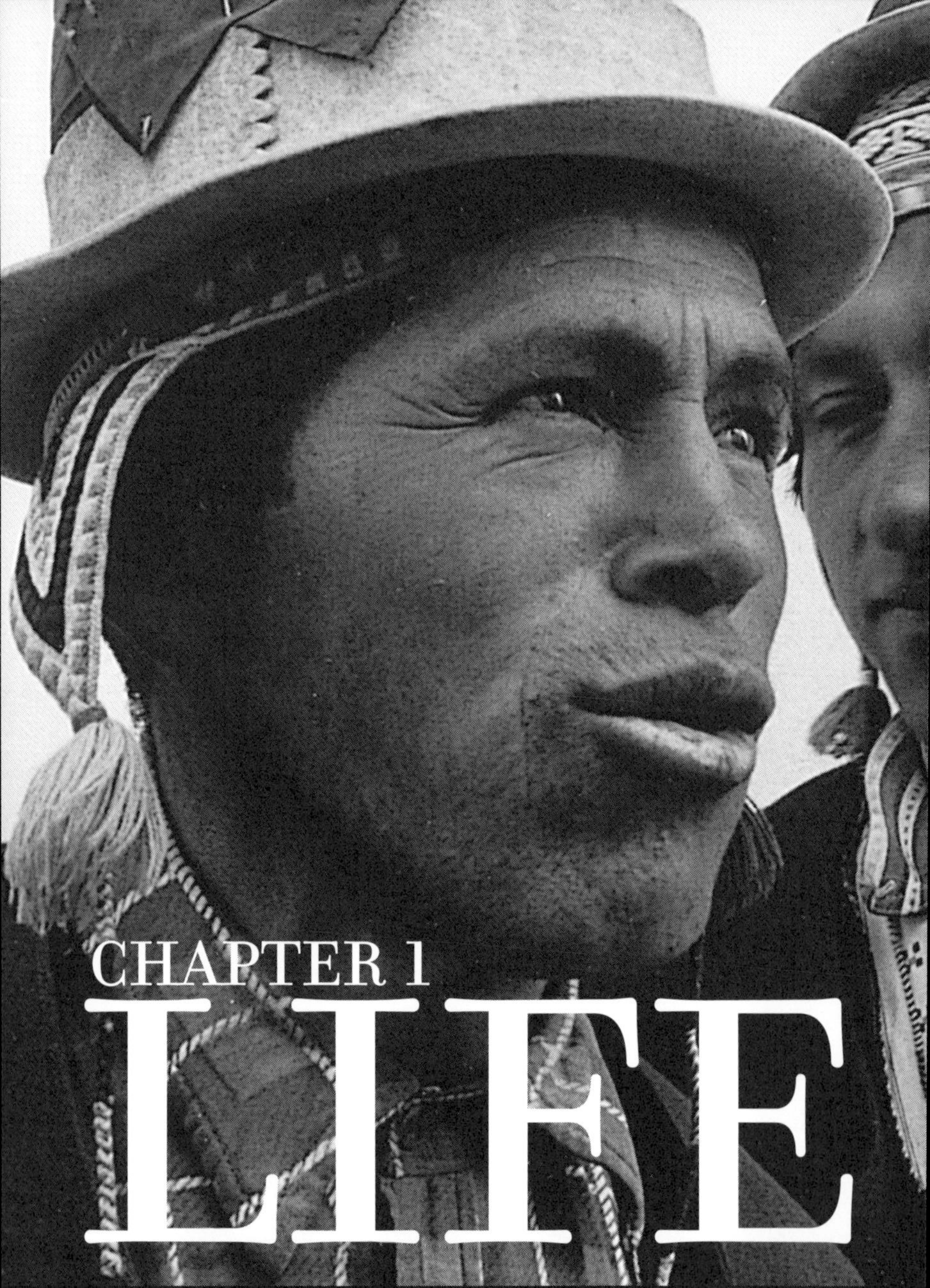

I was born in a place called "Zero Street" in Taiwan and grew up in a shanty there. It was like a cave.

I found out later that it was apparently an air-raid shelter left behind by the former Japanese army.

From the time I was born I had no father, and life was truly poverty-stricken. In Zero Street, many people made their living selling garbage. I used to spend my days there, splashing about in the water naked, playing with stray dogs, stealing water and poaching electricity. I was always hungry, and there were times I felt like catching one of the mice that used to run past me and eating it.

Many people may be surprised to know that all this took place not in some wartime era, but in the 1980s, when the Japanese economy was booming.

I've forgotten most of my memories of that time.

But what I do remember still to this day is my mother saying, "Rich people and poor people all eat the same grain of rice. The time given to them is also completely the same. You have an enormous amount of time left. So it's harder to find a reason for not being able to achieve." She used to say this often and this is all I remember of those days.

I was six years old when I came to Japan; my mother had married again, this time to a Japanese. I'd wanted to escape from my life of poverty, so I was naturally excited at the prospect of a life in affluent Japan.

But what had awaited me was nothing other than terrible discrimination. My classmates used to laugh at the way I talked and even swung punches at me out of the blue, just for being Taiwanese. Such things kept happening over many years, but still, it bothered me. Sometimes I retaliated violently, but that only made the discrimination worse.

Then one day, I came to a realization.

I realized that I am a minority in this country, and this fact was never going to change until the day I died. What's more, in the future, even when I became an adult like everyone else, my past would prove to be an obstacle.

Still, struggling against my surroundings to change them seemed futile. I reasoned that it would be much easier to see myself change — and not in some half-hearted way, either. I wanted to acquire an overwhelming strength that would put me out of reach for anyone's criticism.

If I became stronger, I would surely become liberated and free to pursue whatever I desired with all my heart.

So I resolved to become number one in the world. I was a

teenager then, suffering from the slings and arrows of poverty and discrimination.

I wanted to become number one in the world at something... but at what?

What should I live for?

I spent some time searching for answers to questions like that — questions that really had no answers. But in the end, anything was okay. I just wanted to jump into a world where I could become profoundly excited.

01

Live with meaning.
Die with passion.

When you can't find answers, you tend to feel as if someone else will provide them for you. You're not willing to carve out your own life by yourself. You don't act with self-will, and life keeps passing you by.

Should you just go on leading a life of letting others decide what really matters to you? Or should you start living your own life from this point on?

A life of being constantly afraid of some unidentifiable person, of never being able to gain a firm outlook, is meaningless. Escape from a lukewarm daily existence as soon as possible and start to think about "Why am I alive?", using your own head. Everybody dies. To live means, inevitably, to advance toward death. You may even die tomorrow. But by accepting death in this way, you will become filled with a stronger will to live and feel a resolve to become stronger and take better care of the present.

Don’t live in vain. Live with meaning.

Don't get jerked around by goals made by someone else. Take care of the ones born from your own heart.

And once you make your decision, strengthen your resolve. Everything that occurs to you is because of you.

Whenever you make a decision, to be sure that you don't have complaints later — such as "my partner was bad," "I didn’t have enough time," "if only I’d had a little more money," "I can't come up with any good ideas," "my opinions aren’t being heard" — check to see whether you’d rather give up an arm than quit partway. Cutting off an arm is painful. Would you still be willing to go through with your decision? In confronting your own feelings, be sure to take enough time.

Decide on your own what matters to you.
Do not break promises you make to yourself.

This is the best way to enjoy your life to the fullest.

02

Be conscious of the end.

Rich and poor, young and old, all have to eat to live. They also have the same 24 hours available to them every day. And that's why it's difficult to find a real reason for not being able to achieve.

Still, the reason people fail may often be because they expend energy toward an unclear purpose. Just as with a sea voyage, if you try to cross the ocean without pinpointing the destination, you'll someday run out of steam and become stranded.

We should determine our destination and charge full speed ahead, while we still have plenty of energy left in us.

When you begin to think about the things you need to do in life, if you *add* them up in your mind, inertia sets in, making the fulfillment of your dreams chancy. From the beginning, you should *divide* the time you have remaining in your life and then go about meticulously setting challenges you believe you should accomplish by the end. In clearing them one by one, you'll begin to be filled with the burning realization that you are indeed creating your own future with your own hands.

You can live in the present with intensity simply by being aware of the end.

03

Don't worry.
Don't be afraid of anything.

You fear you might regret getting that job. You wonder if things are really okay the way they are now. You worry that there may be a better way to live. You put a brake on your feelings and hesitate, since you're always afraid of ending up with regrets.

But you really don't need to be afraid of anything... because there are only two kinds of trouble in the world.

One is negative thinking. The other is excessive worrying.

It's always one or the other.

In life, there's very little that is truly worth worrying about. Besides, you won't be able to entirely overcome your fears for the future anyway. At least, not until you're well into your 50s or 60s, when you're old and wise.

The special privilege of youth is not having "infinite possibility," but rather, having the power to fearlessly charge ahead. The more you experience life, the more fears of various kinds you'll come to know. If you have time enough to worry, it would be better to use that time to take immediate action instead.

The strongest enemy you need to confront is the fear that you create for yourself.

There's no use in worrying whether the sun is going to fall from the sky tomorrow. You should never worry over matters over which you have no choice.

04

Do not become dependent. Become a lone lion.

The larger an organization is, the less competent it becomes — and the higher its number of unmotivated workers. This is because they lose the will to make a living on the basis of their own strength. They become blind to the joys of achieving goals by dint of their own efforts, making full use of their hands and feet.

In contrast, in other countries there are people who are risking their lives to gain basic freedoms. Each one of them thinks with their own head and takes action with their own feet, just like a lion.

Lions concentrate all their energy, even if chasing just a rabbit. They do not cut corners.

With such a hunger, you can regain your pride as a person.

If there's a job you want, take the initiative and get it. To be entrusted with the work you want to do, ask for what you want to do, and always win the support and approval of your peers by achieving more targets than others.

Tenacity and persistence are talents in themselves. Knowledge and technique come later.

Have the courage to achieve absolutely on your own, to be convinced that you can. People do help each other out in life, and that's touching. But receiving help like that is not the same thing as allowing yourself to become dependent on others.

05

Be "the nail that sticks out."

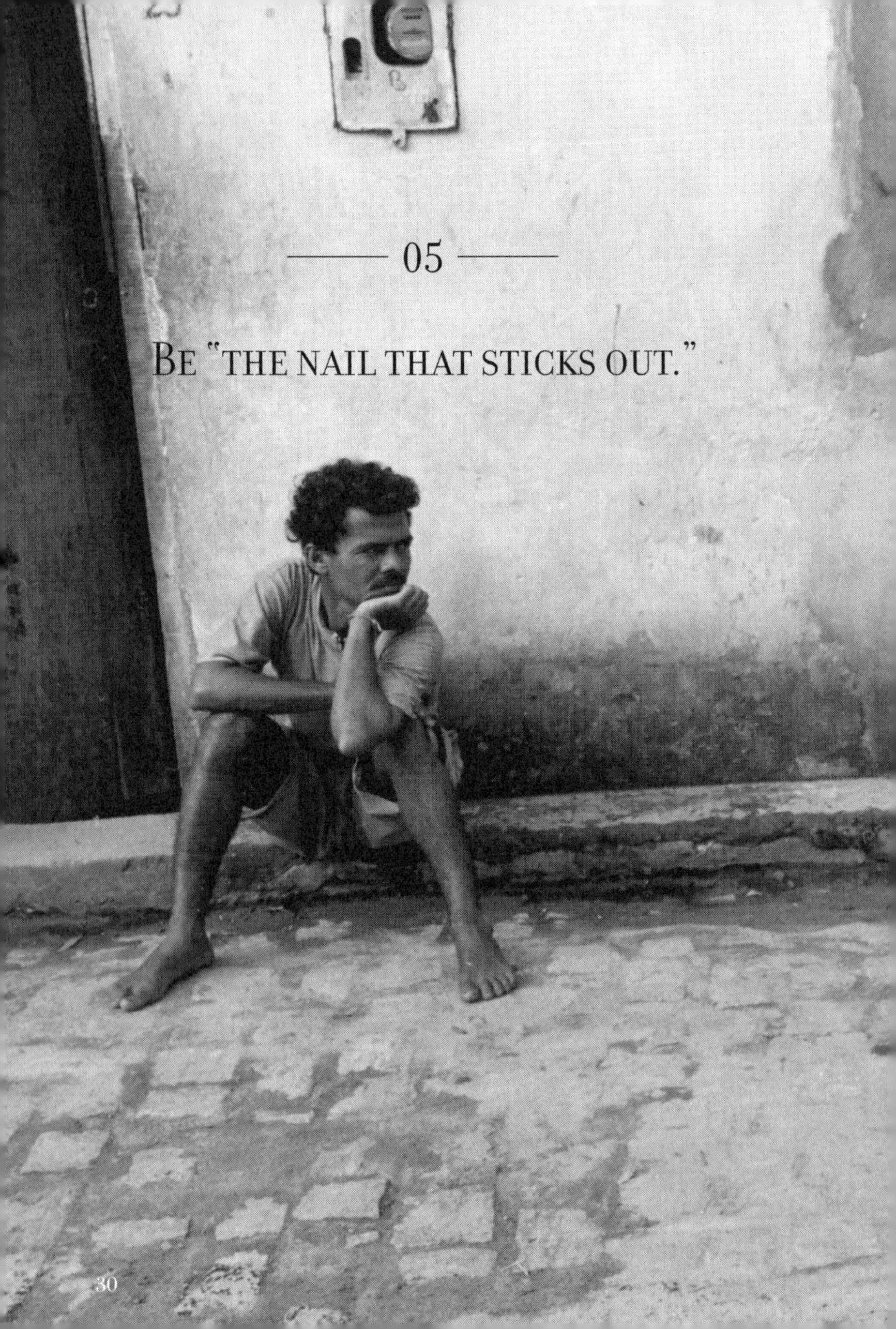

Are you really satisfied with the way things are going? By repeating the same things over and over, day after day, are you not in fact closing your eyes to the fact that if it were up to you, "there would be scope to make a difference"? Try doing what others don't. Dare to become the nail that sticks out. Once you do, you'll open the door to a life of new experiences. Make use of the ordinary expectations of others as a steppingstone to

destroy what is unnecessary in your present life and face new challenges.

You must not be afraid to be different from others. You must also be prepared to be disliked.

It's a risk.

But you can never know your true powers unless you dare to take risks.

Whenever you take an action, just take it at once, intuitively. Don't stop to consider limitations. If you meet with difficulties while changing your circumstances, your action will be all the more worth carrying out.

Express your ideas more freely.

06

Trust your intuition.

Whatever you undertake to do, if you don't have passion, you won't be able to keep going. Passion encourages and delights the people around you and, at times, even gives them reason to idolize you. At the same time, passion serves as a driving force that propels you ever forward toward your ultimate goal. Without passion, you cannot expect to achieve any major success.

But what can you have passion for, in this world?

Only your intuition knows.

The answer is not something you can find simply by wracking your brain or by comparing your standards with those of others.

The only thing you should believe in is your own antenna.

Get involved in anything and everything that moves your spirit. Take up challenges and participate without hesitation. In any case, you'll never know whether you can have passion for something unless you actually try it.

If you keep trying out various things, someday you'll run into something you can be passionate about. To raise the probability of such luck, the best thing you can do is to experience a large number of attempts. By testing your intuitions one after another, you'll begin to nurture critical thinking and ask "why and how" a certain intuition moves you. At the same time, you'll also see a steady rise in the accuracy of your intuition.

0-24
FINE

07

Learn from heroes.

There is a shortcut to success.
To put it simply, the shortcut is to "do your best for whatever is on your plate right now." But this is meaningless if you don't have a burning vision compelling you onward.

So I recommend the hero's road.

Heroes exist in all areas, including sports, business, and politics. Even heroes have heroes. Heroes are linked together in an unbroken chain throughout history.

You also probably have your own hero in mind, someone you aim to be like. Your admiration for what this person does and the desire to emulate this person will prove to help you immensely in improving yourself. I want you to have a ravenous hunger to learn about your hero's life. If you don't know what this entails, I recommend that you put the following into practice as much as possible. Get closer to the hero (physically). Read the hero's biography or autobiography and interviews that appear in magazines or newspapers. Watch videos in which the hero appears. Decorate your room with photographs that show you together with the hero. Buy all available goods related to the hero, and so on.

The more you begin to know about your hero in this way, the more you should begin to see that a hero's life is a series of setbacks and challenges.

The hero you admire may step up in level as you age.

I used to be under the strong influence of a teacher of the martial arts. But at another time, I was moved by the words of Confucius. And at yet another time, I idolized Jun Misugi, a character in the manga "Captain Tsubasa", whose presence tugged at girls' heartstrings, making them constantly concerned over his well-being. Time after time, I kept changing who to idolize.

At present, I'm pretty much settled on Alexander the Great. He was someone who continued to make many wise decisions in an age when life was slow and information was scarce. My visionary ambition right now is to model myself after the image of this leader. In fact, I'd like to outdo him before I die. For this reason, I too must go out into the world.

If you have the ability to deeply admire a hero, you also possess the ability to surpass one. I believe this is so and I'm not ashamed to admit it.

Because, ultimately, no one knows who you will turn out to be in the future.

CHAPTER 2
HEART

After graduating high school, I returned to my native Taiwan and studied there for two years, finding a reaffirmation of my Chinese heritage. In effect, I realized that the tendency "to achieve by dint of your own strength" is strong among Chinese and Taiwanese people. Consequently, I began to think in concrete terms about becoming an entrepreneur.

Upon returning home, I was 20. I decided to make a master plan, which I called "the 50-year plan."

Firstly, in my 20s, establish a company.
In my 30s, make the company No. 1 in its sector in Japan.
In my 40s, make the company No. 1 in its sector in the world.
In my 50s, round the business out.
In my 60s, arrange for the handover of the business to my successors.
In my 70s, spend the remainder of my life engaged in educational and charitable undertakings.

Subsequently, over the course of three years, I educated myself by reading more than 5,000 books on subjects such as management studies, business, and science, and went on to work out a business plan.

At the time, the books that particularly resonated with me were Clear the Way for Destiny by Tenpu Nakamura; Masayoshi Son — The Young Lion of Business, by Eiji Oshita; For the Young Samurai, by Yukio Mishima; and Sanctuary, a work of manga written by Sho Fumimura and illustrated by Ryoichi Ikegami.

Books, to me, are teachers who make me think about how I should live as a human being.

Before long, I resolved to start a biotech business after meeting a graduate student at the place where I worked part time. He was studying about DNA at Tokyo University and opened my eyes to the research that was progressing in the field at the time. Specifically, it was about how available genetic information could be applied to help perceive the state of a person's health and predict the diseases a person might contract in the future. I thought I might be able to find a business application for this technology.

So I went on to draft a business plan revolving around this idea and entered it into a contest sponsored by Kenichi Omae.While there were similar contests elsewhere, I chose his, since Masayoshi Son, someone I greatly respect, was a judge in the contest. I felt strongly that I could get closer to success by making an appeal to him personally.

In this large contest, with over 500 entries, the business plan I proposed fortunately managed to stay in the semifinals for two consecutive years. However, unfortunately, some other team won the grand prize, which was the only financial support offered by the contest.

Nevertheless, I was confident. All I needed were the funds to start up the business. Then one day, when I chanced to drop by a bookstore, I came across a business magazine that had a special feature entitled "The Super Wealthy of Japan."

I became excited looking at the faces of the super-wealthy individuals, whose expressions seemed to suggest that they could see through everything. I also became excited about their positive attitude toward change. But above all, I perceived that I had something in common with the President of Pasona, Mr. Yasuyuki Nanbu. I can't put it into words exactly, but I felt as if his mind-set was akin to mine. In fact, I became convinced that he, above all people, could relate to me and understand my feelings.

Granted, he was someone whose status in life was distant from mine. But I reasoned that nothing was going to happen if I remained timid because of this fact, and that I should begin with what was within my means to do.

So I decided to go and meet him. I thought that if I could only find out his home address, I could somehow get in there and convey my feelings to him. I resolved to hold my ground even if I got threatened or arrested, and in the event I wasn't able to meet him, then I resolved to die.

I seem to have been a pretty good stalker, if I do say so myself. I telephoned ten times every day in the hope of somehow catching his attention. While the secretary who answered the phone was kind enough to say, "I'll at least convey your feelings," all I kept saying was "Please, please let me meet him!" Since there were times I was recognized and cut off immediately, I sometimes used a falsetto voice and pretended to be another person.

This went on back and forth for a full week. Finally—perhaps my persistence had paid off— I succeeded in eliciting from Mr. Nanbu the response "Interesting, I'll allow a meeting."

What I wanted to show Mr. Nanbu was my business plan and mission statement. I also intended to convey that I was ready to risk my life for the business, and that I was not going to spare any effort in investing my body and soul toward this end.

But a person accustomed to dealing in hundreds of billions of yen was not going to be in the least interested by my plans and declarations unless I presented myself in a "radical" way. So I went on to slit my finger with a knife in order to stamp a seal of blood (and made my friends do the same as well, much to their reluctance). I was ready for anything.

As it turned out, all it took for President Nanbu to tell me "I'll support you" was not the business plan, but just one look at the blood-sealed petition.

So I succeeded in acquiring a powerful supporter and obtained financing, and became absolutely convinced that my business was going to make it. However, at the same time, I had begun to perceive a gap between the biotech business and the times we were living in then. I thought that it was still too early. While technically feasible, the business itself was not recognized by the world, so it would have been a difficult task to make viable the services that biotech had to offer.

Then too, I was not all that comfortable with the half-hearted attitudes of my peers, who still seemed to behave like students. In this world called business, there are many people who work over ten hours every day. We were already losing in terms of such drive. So I asked them: "Should we continue our research in a lackadaisical manner like students, or should we choose to treat this like a real job?"

When I pressed them for an answer, unfortunately, they all opted to go on living like students.

While all this was going on, a woman I knew passed away. Just like me, she was half Taiwanese and had grown up in a fatherless family. As it happens, she was also my first love. Her mother was grief-stricken and exhausted, so I took care of the funeral arrangements for her.

At the funeral, during the recitation of the sutras, the commemorative photo appeared to be displayed at an angle, but no one had even tried to straighten it. Even the undertaker was no help at all, reproaching me that doing so would interfere with the funeral service. I learned intense rage at that moment, wondering for whom in the world this funeral was being carried out in the first place. And that rage gradually turned into a zeal for overturning the funeral industry from its very foundations.

08

Use the fluctuations of your heart as a springboard.

A woman I knew passed away. Just like me, she was half Taiwanese and had grown up in a fatherless family. As it happens, she was also my first love. Her mother was grief-stricken and exhausted, so I took care of the funeral arrangements for her.

At the funeral, during the recitation of the sutras, the commemorative photo appeared to be displayed at an angle, but no one had even tried to straighten it. Even the undertaker was no help at all, reproaching me that doing so would interfere with the funeral service. I learned intense rage at that moment, wondering for whom in the world this funeral was being carried out in the first place. And that rage gradually turned into a zeal for overturning the funeral industry from its very foundations.

In this way, a major emotion can at times become the driving force toward taking new action.

If you cannot find your purpose in life, then look back to your past and try to recall events or moments that moved you deeply. Ask yourself these questions: Who did I want to be like? What stirred my soul? Where did my strengths show? What did I immerse myself in? What did I find unforgivable? How was I different from others? By recalling such apparently trivial events in your past, you may begin to see a new purpose for yourself.

A purpose is not something you create.
It's something you remember.

In your past, there were certain moments in which you did certain things that made you very happy and helped you to get in close touch with yourself. Happily, all your dreams spring from such moments in your life.

MOIS

09

Dare to jump into difficult situations.

It's after you fail that you gain know-how for the first time. This is because unless you face what's wrong with you, unless you confront what it is about you that causes inconvenience for or troubles others, you won't be able to plan your next move.

When you take up challenges, at times you'll find yourself in difficulties. But difficulties don't last forever.

If you try to escape them, difficulties will likely dog you all the more. If you choose to ignore a problem and avoid dealing with it when it's at an early stage, you run the risk of someday being dealt a mortal wound, instead of a minor scratch.

Wary of damaging their self-esteem, many people fear to fail. But such people are incapable of creating anything worthwhile. And since they're aware of this fact, they turn a critical eye on all those who are ambitious about new things. It's truly a vicious circle.

Avoid becoming an obstinate and inflexible human being. If you see the opportunity to jump into a difficult situation, go ahead and take it. If you find a project that seems difficult, or rigorous duties that need to be done, volunteer to do them.

Failure will teach you about many things. Success, after all, is an extension of failure.

The greatest failure is avoiding challenges for fear of failure.

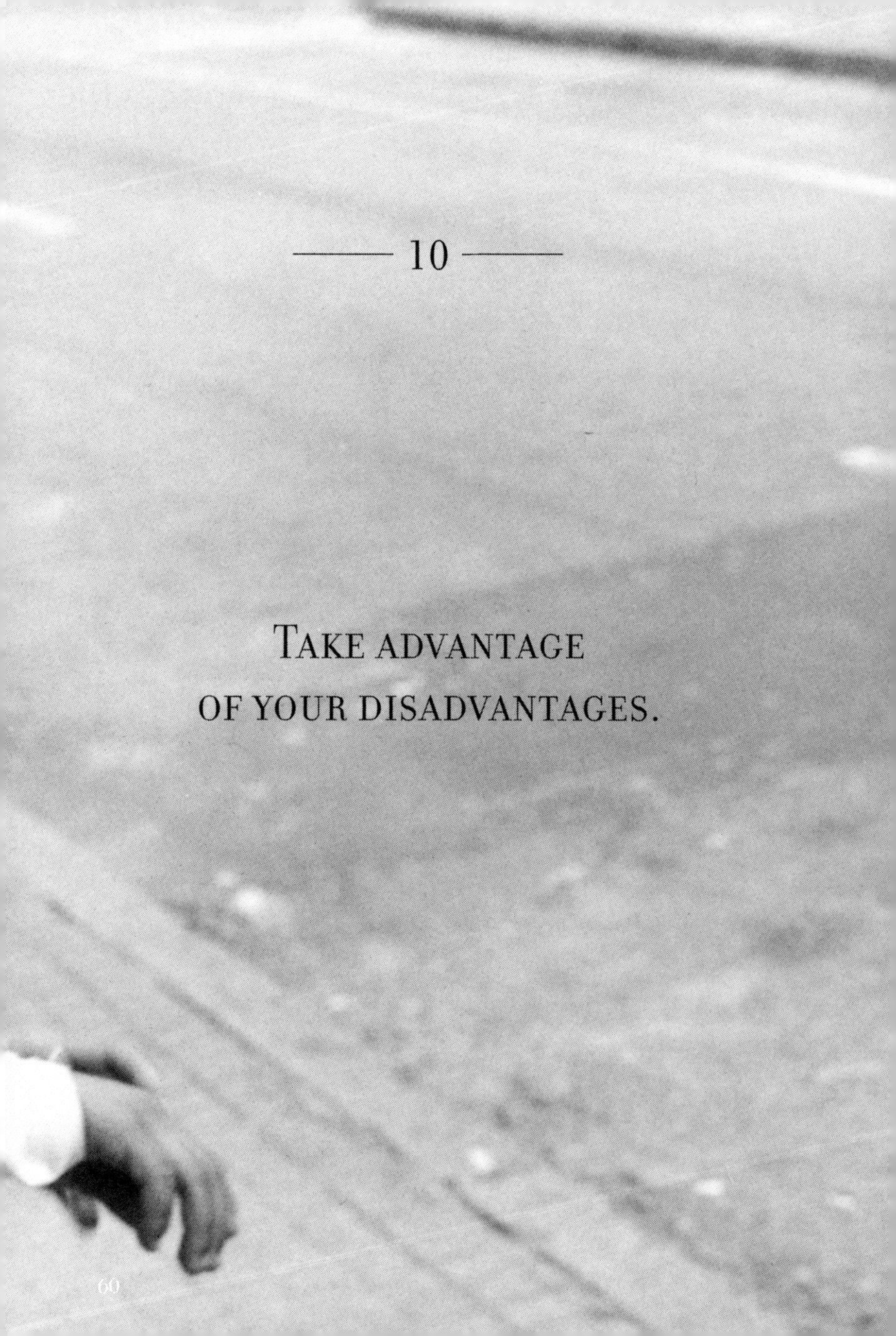

10

TAKE ADVANTAGE OF YOUR DISADVANTAGES.

Advantages and disadvantages are one and the same.

The brighter side of having a nervous temperament and worrying over details is that you may very well be very careful about your work. Seen in a positive light, a person who is stubborn and tends to become strongly attached to people and things is also possibly tenacious and strong-willed. An illness disables your body and distorts your feelings to no end. If possible, it's certainly preferable to prevent or even eliminate it. But there are times when becoming ill helps you to realize, on a profound level, just how wonderful life can be. Even illnesses have their upsides and reasons for occurring.

It's easy to fix a shortcoming you don't like. All you need to do is make use of that shortcoming for the good of others. In other words, you should make use of it in a way that pleases people. By doing so, they will come to recognize your shortcoming as your strength.

Anyone has the innate ability to change shortcomings into strengths.

But too many people don't realize this.

You should invest your energy not into fixing your shortcomings by force, but into applying them in the service of people who approve of them as your strengths.

PUERTO

11

GIVE 100% TO WHATEVER IS ON YOUR PLATE AT THE MOMENT.

To do or not to do... Life is about making choices. But it doesn't really matter what choice you make.

What really counts is what action you take after making your choice. That's what determines the value of your choice. At any rate, as long as you're prepared to make choices, you won't go wrong, because whether you choose A or B, it will all go well in the end.

What we view as "destiny" is often just a conclusion based on hindsight. When you look back at what has already happened, you tend to think that it was destined to happen.

Additionally, the question of whether your choice was good or bad is entirely subjective. Whatever your feelings tell you will always be the correct answer.

When the future is unclear, give 100% to whatever you've chosen to do in the here and now.

Even if you're only able to take small steps, don't be discouraged. Just keep going. You become anxious when you become stationary. If you stay in motion, it's certain that, sooner or later, your circumstances will suddenly become brighter. There's never any time to think about turning back.

— 12 —

TAKE RISKS.

From the beginning, it's best not to depend on others. Accomplish your aims as much as possible by yourself.

Any guy who forces others to do what he doesn't want to do himself is a loser.

When I established my company at the age of 25, I raised funds entirely by myself, without any help from investors. I borrowed about 7 million yen from consumer credit companies. (Since I had neither the requisite experience nor collateral, I didn't even consider borrowing from banks or government-run financial institutions.) Before it came to light that I was a multiple debtor, I made rounds to several of these companies in one day and ended up incurring a 24% interest risk.

I took this route to financing because I didn't want others to have to pay the costs before I did. If I'd let them do that, I'd never have been able to forgive myself. Also, to hope for the sudden appearance of investors or angels seemed fainthearted, and I felt that I wouldn't be able to persevere with such an attitude; I was sure I'd become dependent on the kindness of others. And that way lies ruin, since people tend to give up easily the things they obtain easily.

Later, when I incurred debt, I prepared myself for the worst and felt an exhilarating tension run through me. That tension eventually helped the yearly turnover of my company grow to 3 billion yen (as of December 2005).

The royal road to success is about taking risks with more pleasure than anyone else.

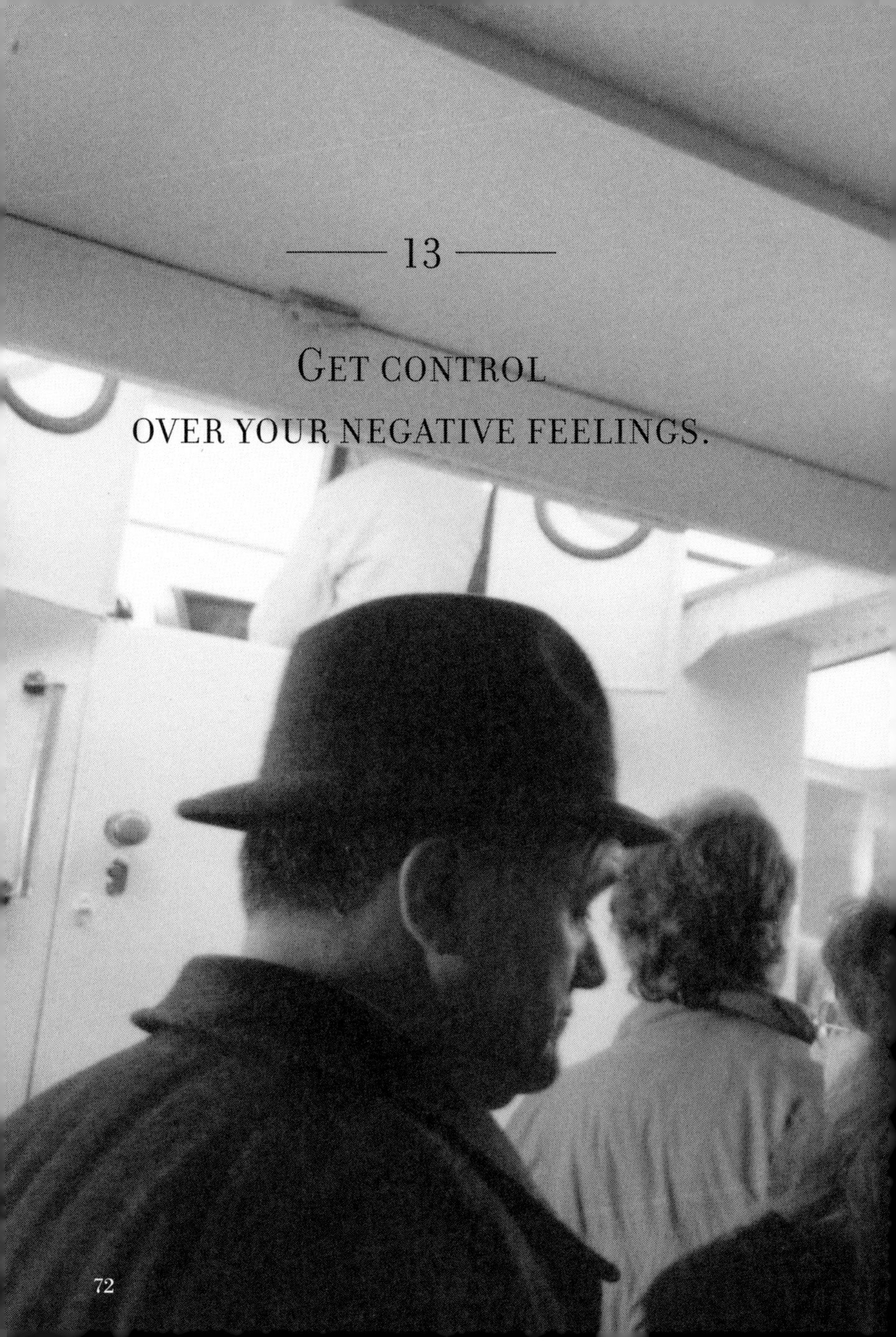

13

Get control over your negative feelings.

If you had a map and a compass, you'd be able to reach Treasure Island even if you had to crawl all the way there yourself.

But when all is said and done, even the best among us will turn into naysayers and call such a feat impossible. They'll often find they can't get all the necessary funds, tools, and staff beforehand. So even before failing, they'll already have an excuse for it.

If you're going to put a brake on yourself like that, you'd be better off doing nothing at all.

What's important is to get a grip on your negative feelings and take control by dint of sheer willpower.

If you can't do that, you will have no control over your actions in the future as well.

The map you need to make your dreams come true is a set of plans and schedules, while the compass you need is a set of personal principles and concepts. With these under your belt, all you need to do next is

immediately take a step forward. Whatever else you need will follow without a hitch.

In my case, I make a point of translating my plans into action any time that I become convinced I could go at least 70% of the way. This is because if I waited any longer, I know I'd definitely miss the best timing.

It's fun to stir yourself into action. It's even more fun to be able to appreciate yourself in action.

14

Choose a place
that you find comfortable.

When you begin something new, choose your point of departure carefully.

For me, the criteria for selecting a place depend more on whether it's comfortable than on whether it can help in promoting business success.

Simply put, if it's a place I like, I'll feel uplifted and will also be spared unnecessary stress. And I'll find it easy to find inspiration there.

When starting up my company, I decided that it should have a Roppongi address. I simply believed that was the cool thing to do. However, on my budget at that time, finding a place in Roppongi meant that my only choice would be a low-rent apartment. On top of that, people advised me that the interior and furnishings would by no means be good.

Before long, though, I got word of a vacancy in a public housing property. Both the location and the terms were optimal. But the room faced west, so I declined the offer. I was adamant about getting a room facing east with a view of the Tokyo Tower, which I'm crazy about. Then, fortunately, the very next day I was informed of a vacancy for a room facing east, on the 16th floor of a 20-story building. And that's where I went on to form the company.

Is there anything odd about this episode?

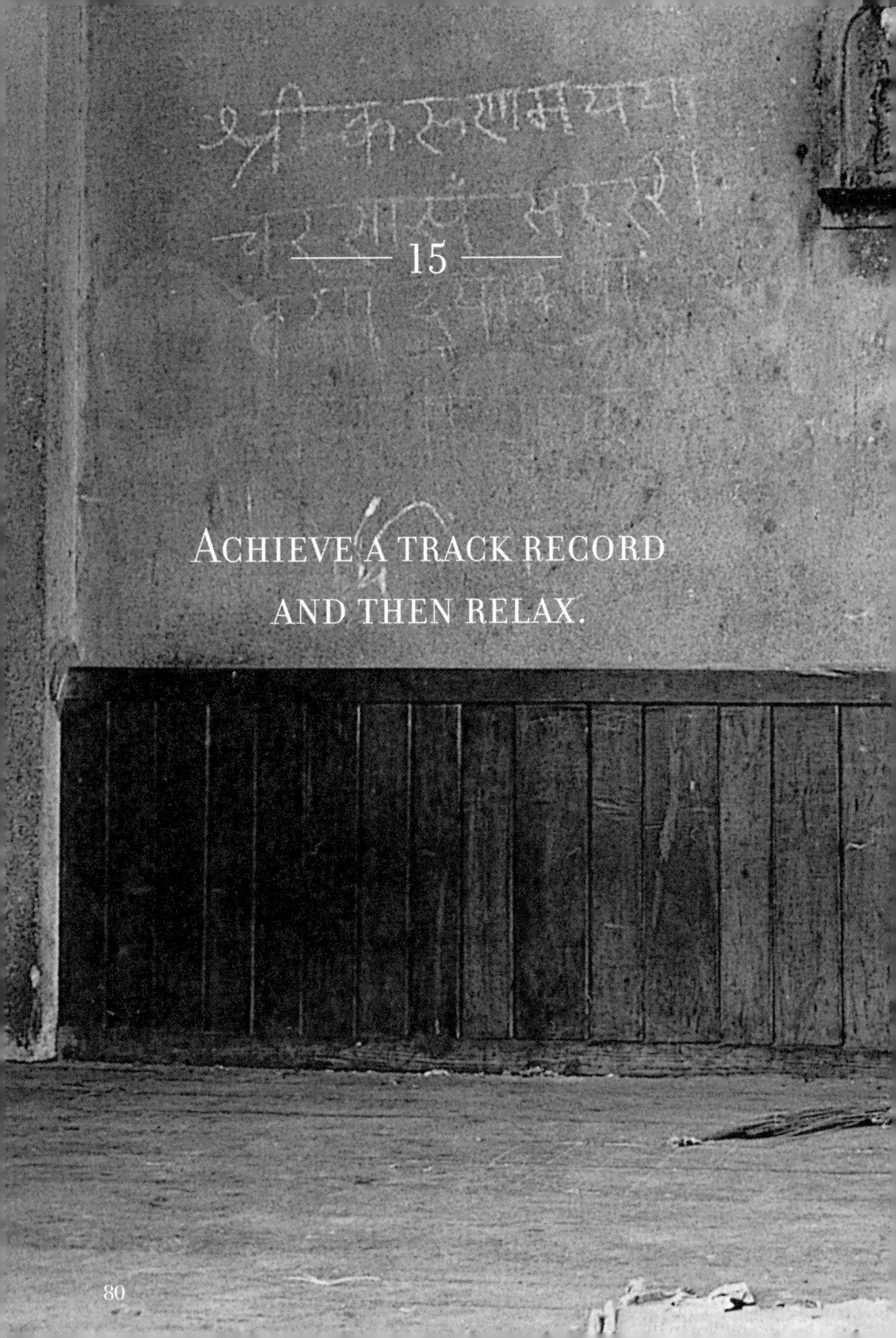

15

Achieve a track record and then relax.

Attain a track record early, to prevent giving others any reason to reject you. Having a track record is much simpler than having to figure out how to go about persuading people.

New proposals will usually make people defensive, or put them off, or possibly both.

At the least, they won't be able to arrive at any judgments through your explanations alone. It's not easy to find people who will promise their loyalty to you and offer money and opportunities for things that they don't understand.

First and foremost, you have to show a track record that can be viewed as established fact and be easily appreciated by others.

It must be readily apparent that this track record could only have been achieved through immensely challenging endeavors.

Successful people tend to immediately seek out the roots of their problems and actively try to eliminate them. If your problem is a lack of trust from others, all you need to do is begin working toward producing a remarkable track record. This is the best shortcut.

I realize that this is difficult. If it were simple, everyone would be doing it.

But due to the very fact that it is difficult for everyone, it's worth your while to make an attempt yourself.

16

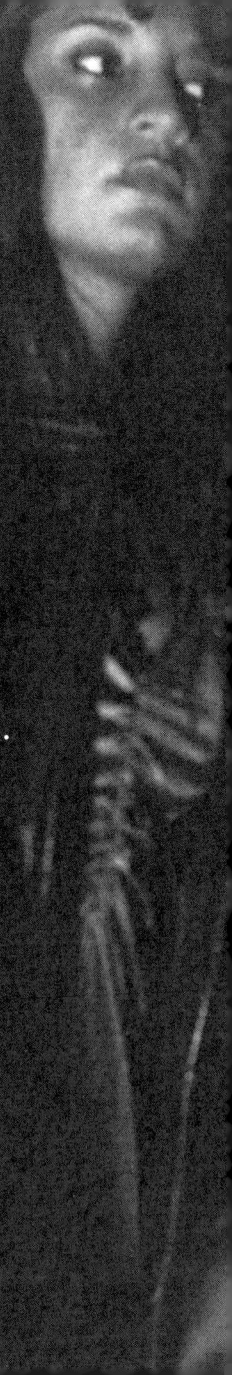

IF YOU LOSE YOUR WAY,
STRENGTHEN YOUR RESOLVE.

In life, moments will arise when you should stake your all on a gamble.

In such situations, your past achievements won't matter in any way. You will, in effect, find yourself in an all-or-nothing world.

Still, if you throw yourself into your work, the road ahead will become clear.

To convey that you're willing to risk your life, spare no effort, and devote your entire body and soul for your work, you must have a certain sense of "manic compulsion." It doesn't matter if you get ridiculed or even arrested. You may have to get down on your knees, some of your own blood, sit in front of doors, and even risk your health. But such a single-minded and frank way of life will be the key to changing your destiny.

It's no use being satisfied with halfhearted attempts. An old Japanese adage says, "You can float in rapids only when you abandon yourself to the currents." This means that you'll be able to escape from predicaments only when you take yourself to the limit.

There is no decision greater than the one made with a sense of profound preparedness. If you lose your way, be prepared to die.

You will die right here, right now, if that is your destiny. If you have matters left undone, you will not die.

It's up to divine providence.

17

WHAT YOU CAN ACHIEVE,
ONLY YOU CAN KNOW.
STAND YOUR GROUND.

For many, getting along well with the people around them is a top priority. But at the same time, realizing what they want to do for themselves is important as well. Naturally, to be loved by all is a wonderful thing. But unfortunately, a person who aims to rise above the status quo can't hope to be a philanthropist at the same time.

At times, there will be some who'll say, "That's impossible, it's bound to be futile." Others will recommend putting things off, saying, "It's a hassle; let's do it next time." There will even be those who take a critical attitude and try to hold you back whenever you attempt something new.

If you try to meet the demands of all such people, your faith in yourself will wear out in no time.

"Whatever people of this world may say, only I know what I can achieve." These were the words left behind by Sakamoto Ryoma when he was a teenager. He was a man who absolutely refused to listen to the voices of opposition, no matter how much slander he had to suffer as a result.

You must not lend your ear to noise.
Once you make a decision, follow it through to the end with absolute determination.

The person who understands you the best is none other than yourself. To lie to yourself, to become disliked by yourself, those are the greatest tragedies of all.

Do not shake the axis of your being. If the trunk snaps, neither the branches nor the leaves will have value anymore.

CHAPTER 3
CHANGE

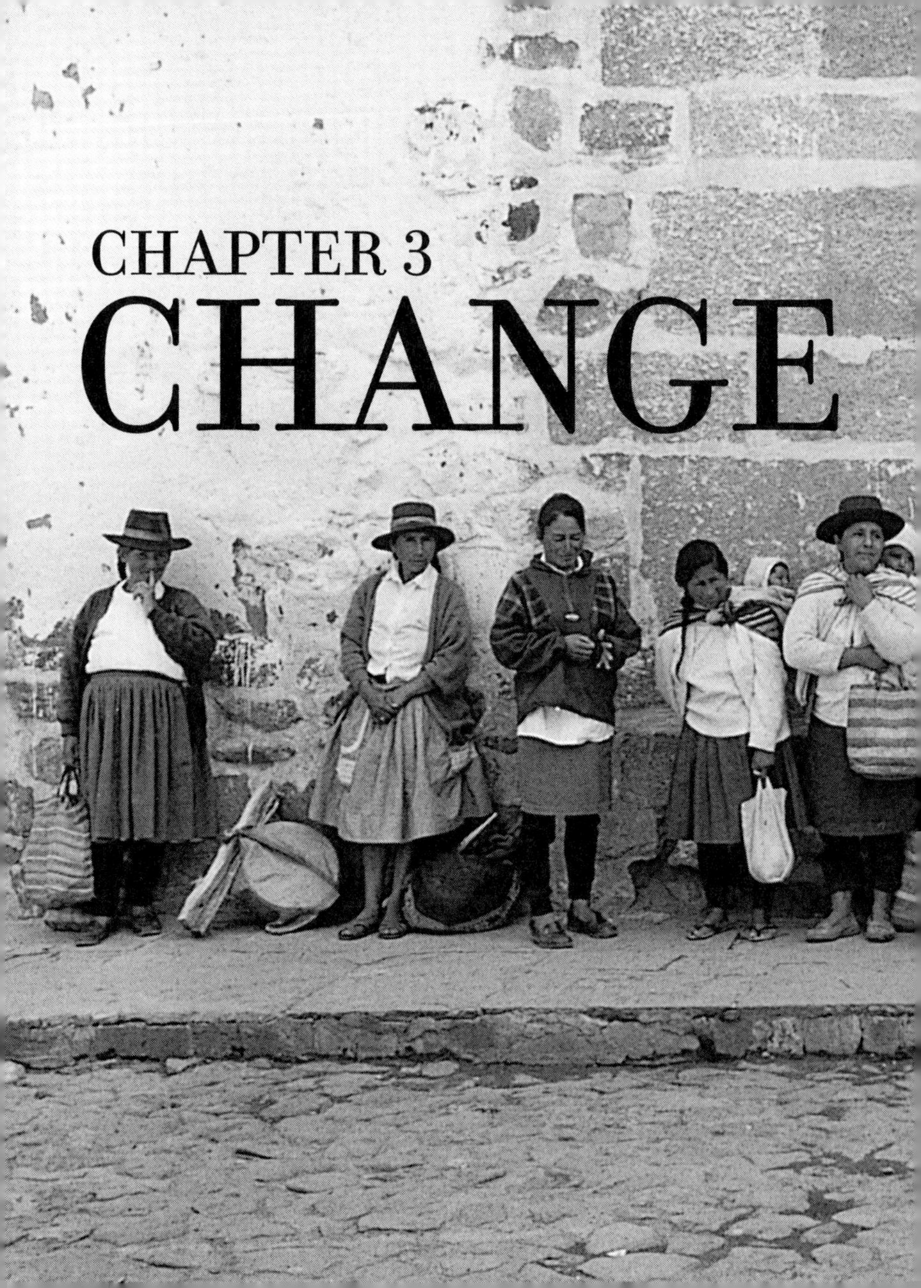

BLACK
STEEL

Having made up my mind to make fundamental changes in Japan's funeral service business, I set about to research and analyze that entire industry.

Consequently, I found that community-based, small-scale companies accounted for the majority. Despite the large market, only a few major companies were involved. In addition, there were many obscure aspects about the trade's pricing practices and services, and the companies suffered from a forbidding, underground image.

Since I had neither grounding nor know-how in the field, I literally went down on my knees to plead with a certain funeral service firm to hire me. I ended up working there for a while, but quit soon after becoming disillusioned by the company's preoccupation with competing on the basis of price alone.

Nevertheless, I became convinced that if that was the case, the prospects for success were good for me as well. Two months after resigning, I had established Sanctuary Corporation.

A funeral service is something that will be required again, sooner or later, within the family of the departed. But there are times when it's not possible to conduct a funeral actually in the home. For such cases, I felt the least I could do was offer a service that would help the bereaved feel as relaxed as if they were in their own home. With such a goal, I launched the "House Ceremony" brand.

I believe that, in their lifetime, an average person acts as the chief mourner in a funeral two or three times at most. For this reason, the public generally does not know the market price of a funeral service. Taking advantage of this fact, traditional funeral service companies fixed the basic charge cheaply on purpose so that they could jack up their ultimate price by attaching one option after another. Also, though a gratuity to the priest is considered a discretionary matter, they tacitly demanded a specific amount of money above a certain level.

So I took it upon myself to show, upfront, all details involved in the sum totals of funeral-service expenses. I went on to standardize the amount of the token to the priest. Also, compared to the excessive 60 to 70 percent taken by conventional funeral service companies, I was able to hold down my gross-profit margin to around 30 percent.

However, this way of dong business resulted in a backlash. From the start, funeral service companies had never been very open to newcomers. They'd long enjoyed a cozy give-and-take relationship with the "entry and exit merchants" of hospitals. I hadn't joined this general network, so I had a hard time acquiring projects.

One time, at an annual funeral service forum, a sign was placed at the venue's entrance that read "The Naoe Family Funeral Service Ceremonial Hall." This was open harassment.

Nevertheless, ten months after the launching of my company the first funeral service turned out to be deeply impressive.

It was not the conventional, ordinary type of funeral service. It was secular, fully customized, and heartfelt.

We decorated with the roses that the departed liked, prepared a pretty cake, and played nostalgic music. We also showed memorable scenes with a projector. As for the commemorative photo, we used a gorgeous one, which looked like the cover of a fashion magazine. The funeral turned into something truly cheerful, like a wedding.

After the ceremony, several of the bereaved remarked, "It was a wonderful farewell." As I bowed to them, I felt a joy that seemed to well up from the tips of my toes. I was truly glad to have undertaken it.

One day, suddenly there must be a funeral. Without having the time to grieve properly, the bereaved must contact acquaintances and make arrangements for a hearse, a token to the priest, food, and reciprocal gifts.

But grief is the same for all families. I don't think there is any place more universal than one where a funeral is performed.

By virtue of my work, I coexist with death. For this reason perhaps, I strongly feel that leading your life is like dressing up for death. Who knows: I may die tomorrow. But I believe that the act of accepting death gives rise to the desire to live strongly in the present and to try to live without regrets. I believe it heightens your will to live.

There may be people who don't want to think about such things. Nevertheless, death is inevitable and visits us all. At least, I don't want to live in vain. I want to live with meaning, and die with passion. That's how I feel.

My journey – which I began in Japan with a firm resolve to become the world's best businessman, after clawing my way up from a shanty in Taiwan – still continues. While the distance I need to cover to achieve this end is considerable, by no means do I believe that it's insurmountable. I will change things, and I seriously believe that I can become number one in the world. I may collapse in the course of the journey someday. But since I've been able to dash to where I am today by giving my all, I don't think I'll ever have any regrets.

18

Peace is dangerous. Enjoy change.

Correo
CAE HUGO CHAVEZ
Tenia su propio cartel
CASAS DE DOS PISOS A 94 SOLES
Perú
Buena Salud
CONTRAGOLPE
Buena Salud
Buena Salud

All things flow and nothing is permanent. Everything that exists in this world is in a state of constant flux, movement, and change.

A peaceful life does not continue forever. If all you're doing right now to maintain your present lot in life is praying, you're being negligent. Trying to avoid change is the same thing as renouncing your self-will. You may have already become tightly knit with an organization or your group of friends; but remember this:

No matter how comfortable your present circumstances, they will one day change in unimaginable ways.

So even when you feel everything is going smoothly, you should hope to be blessed with more future opportunities that will allow you to aim higher.

As for matters of low priority, you need to have the courage to be able to just abandon them. Once you do that, your heart will open up to new ideas.

When my company began to see a growth in sales, I did not increase the number of employees. With the fear of losing flexibility through becoming too big, I felt more comfortable, instead, in partnering with adept dealers and turning the company into a brand. For the first three years after its inception, I kept changing the business model every year to adapt to changing circumstances. If things had gone awry, the company might have gone bankrupt, but fortunately it grew by leaps and bounds and its scope expanded as well.

Rather than being afraid that your surroundings will change, bring about change on your own and take pleasure in it.

Even the waters of the river get muddy when they cease to flow. The beauty of water is that it always continues to flow.

19

THERE ARE NO DRAWBACKS.
EVEN IF THERE ARE, IGNORE THEM.

Ignore everything negative.

If you think something is hopeless, it really will become hopeless.

You don't need to regain what you lack. Whether you analyze your drawbacks or apply yourself to your next task, the amount of time you invest is the same. Regard the present as your point of origin, and begin. The situation will definitely take a turn for the better. That's how it has always been.

In the end, there will always be a happy ending.
Reset your mind with this affirmation and start moving forward now.

As for generally negative people who are prone to criticize, slander, become jealous, and make excuses, you should cut off your ties with them — at the very least, in your mind. It's better that you consider whatever they say to be nothing more than their personal opinion, no matter how important they may sound. In addition, you don't need to take the trouble to try to understand them if it means having to suppress your own feelings in the process. Just say, "I well understand what you said, but I don't agree," and leave. This approach will very likely serve the best interests of both parties for the future.

There are no drawbacks. Such things do not exist.

If there are, you are simply creating them on your own.

20

Play with all your heart. Forget stress.

Is your mind healthy? Are you taking care of it properly?

No matter how strong-willed you are, if you continue to accumulate stress, your body will one day break down. There is no human being with zero stress (except for a baby in the mother's womb), but the problem arises when you fail to release stress, and allow it to accumulate.

If possible, you should seek to eliminate the root causes of stress. More often than not, though, you'll generally be at a loss if you attempt to do so on your own. It would be nice if an irritable boss, an incompetent subordinate, or a stubborn client were to just disappear, but things don't readily take care of themselves in such a way.

What is important is to change your way of thinking about stress. I don't try to get rid of stress. I just engage in pleasurable activities that overwhelmingly compensate for my stress. I play and play and keep playing, and try everything from A to Z that interests me. Thanks to this attitude, whenever I feel stress now, I just get all the more excited, feeling a competitive and rebellious spirit grow inside me.

Unless the balance between tension and relaxation is retained, human beings become depressed.

Make a point of reserving time to play with all your heart.

Toward this end, be sure to finish things that should be done, within the time you set aside for them.

SERRALHEIRO
SOLDA ELÉTRICA

21

Stay calm.
There is no crisis
that is insurmountable.

When a sudden crisis strikes, your mind turns blank, doesn't it?

Well, not mine. This is because I regularly imagine myself in emergencies and mentally go through the actions I need to take in such situations. In other words, I carry out simulations in my mind.

I wonder, "What if a big earthquake strikes? What if the police arrest me? What if I almost get murdered? Or what if I fail to manage the company's financing?"

When I was very young, there was a time I pretended to have suddenly lost my eyesight, and consequently spent my days blindfolded in a pitch-black room.

Gradually, I became desensitized to crisis situations, and had even begun to fall under the illusion that I was almost invincible. It was as if I'd become absorbed in some virtual-reality game and couldn't tell reality from fiction. But I don't in any way believe this to be a good thing. In fact, I don't want you to become like me in this way at all. It's just that I simply enjoy stimulating simulations more than other people do on average.

To understand what a crisis really is you have to experience it, not just speculate about it. This is common sense. But before a crisis happens to you, I'd like you to understand that

there is no crisis that you will ever have to face that you cannot overcome by yourself.

While you may find yourself in a situation where a product you'd ordered hasn't arrived, you will never find yourself in a situation where someone complains to you to do something about the world economy.

All problems that befall you contain the seeds of their own solution, which can be found once you calm down and think about them.

Having said that, even I have experienced a time when my mind went blank — once. It happened at a briefing session about my company that took place very soon after it was established. It dawned on me that the venue had become filled to capacity, and moreover, that more than 70 percent of the attendees were women. I was moved and became teary-eyed and speechless. That was an unexpected happening.

— 22 —

Feel the weight of love.

The grief of losing someone is the same in all families. The last moments are wrapped in the warmth of family and friends and become sublimated into spirit.

Anywhere in the world, the sorrow for the death of a person does not change. It is universal. After becoming involved in the funeral business, I've become ever more aware of the profound weight of love.

When you lose someone close to you, there are aspects of that person you come to value for the first time. You don't want to regret, in hindsight, that you hadn't done more of one thing or another for them.

Cherish the people you love, always.

— 23 —

Become intoxicated with yourself.

Your physique will suddenly begin to lose shape. You must not begin to resemble the kind of person you told yourself as a child that you never wanted to look like. If you stop paying attention to the way you look for even a little while, you'll put on a potbelly, your back will get rounded, and you'll begin to dress shabbily, turning into the kind of unsightly person who sighs and complains of being tired all the time.

I want you to pay maximum attention to your style.

Both your appearance and your personality are important factors that will reflect on your work.

Here are some affirmations I want you to try:

I want to be cool.

I want to lead a cool lifestyle.

It doesn't matter if others think I'm a narcissist.

Try to say them to yourself on a regular basis, looking into a mirror. And keep imagining your figure in its best condition. The more serious you are about your ideal figure, the closer your actual physique will approach it. If you start to gain weight and get flabby, you should become thoroughly critical with yourself until you return to your healthier state. Don't give up partway, and don't take a so-what attitude. This is not just your problem. After all,

improving your appearance is an act of consideration for all the people you keep company with.

I believe this to be true.

When one becomes content with the status quo and starts to take it easy, there is no limit to how unsightly one can become. Life is like a lotus flower. You want to always live with beauty.

24

Vitalize your body on a regular basis.

If your body is healthy, your mind will be too. Your ability to concentrate will increase and you'll be able to manage two to three times more work than usual. You may find this painful to hear, but for the wage-earning professional, I believe that carrying out decent health care is an act of courtesy toward your employer. It's the least you could do to show respect for them.

Let me tell you about my daily routine.

Since I was twenty, I've been waking up every morning at half past four. The days I don't get out of bed at this time are the days I lose out. (When I was not used to rising early, I used to dash cold water on my face.) Immediately after waking up, I do meditation for 15 minutes and then take a shower.

During this time, I finish making decisions for the work completed up to yesterday and also finish most of my scheduling for the entire day. I jot down and organize any thoughts that occur to me in a notebook. From five to six o'clock, I send out instructions to the company by e-mail. This is because, early in the morning, my mind is clear and I'm less likely to make some error in judgment.

In my case, eating a full breakfast makes my blood rush down to my stomach, making my brain less alert, so I always have a light breakfast, taking only protein in liquid form. I cannot part with my glass of water. If I don't have water, I'm useless. I drink two liters every day without fail. I eat a normal lunch and dinner. But I don't smoke cigarettes; I drink liquor only in moderation, and only when necessary.

Before going to sleep, I try to keep my stomach as empty as possible. When I bathe, I take a half-body bath (that is, hot water level only up to the waist). For 30 minutes, I perform yoga and stretches. This is the time I touch base with my instincts. I stretch out my body until I attain a level of comfort, and let my imagination run far and wide. Then, as in the morning, I meditate for 15 minutes. This feels really good.

I do the meditation to New Age music, in a pitch-dark room. I inhale for seven seconds, hold for seven seconds, and exhale for seven seconds, while visualizing the vibrations of a positive consciousness coming together from the earth and the universe. I see these vibes well up inside me, wash away the bad vibes, and then course through my entire body, slowly reaching my heart in the end.

Then I begin to see an image that commands a view of my entire life. Firstly, I imagine my own death in vivid detail. From there, like a video rewinding, I trace back to when age 60, 50, 40, 30, and so on. Then, at precisely the 15th minute, I return to my present self.

The reason I'm not interested in hot spring baths and massages is that my own practices, as outlined above, allow me to attain adequate relaxation before I settle into sleep, which is at midnight every night.

JUNTO A

25

STUDY AND PRACTICE.

Every morning, I spend about 30 minutes catching up on the news from the newspaper and the Internet. Then I read special-interest magazines that I subscribe to. I can't say much for television as a medium of information, since what you end up receiving contains so many items you really couldn't care less about.

As for reading books, if possible, you should strike a balance between those that help to raise your level of knowledge and those that help to improve your skills. If you concentrate, your reading speed will be fast. Like a school's class schedule, I set aside time separately for different subjects, including management, technology, and philosophy. If you read with a theme in mind, you will avoid getting distracted by unnecessary thoughts.

Carry out your studies systematically as well. For the first 10 minutes of a 60-minute study cycle, think about what you're trying to learn. Spend the next 20 minutes reading the book (input). Devote the remaining 20 minutes to problem solving (output). Then take a 10-minute break.

Optimize your study results through the way you study, rather than using sheer brainpower. Most brilliant people exchange with each other not only knowledge but also effective learning methods.

One such way is to create "a perfect reference book" for you alone to use. If information is scattered, things could get confusing; but when it can be all found concentrated in one place, learning becomes easy. I came to understand that, in essence, this reference book — or master book, if you will — can serve as a sort of central repository for one's knowledge. Even memorizing just its contents could easily enhance your education.

Copy down into your master book entire chunks of information from reference books and other books. If you do this on a subject-specific basis, you'll learn rapidly. Remember, the more you read, the more perfect your master book can become.

But a person's memory can be unreliable. No matter how earnestly you try to learn something, come tomorrow you will have forgotten about half of it. As we were taught in school, so it is today: reviewing is essential. Even if you have only two to three minutes to spare, you should review periodically: a week later, a month later, three months later, six months later.

What's more, compared to reading a book once at a slow and careful pace over the course of a single day, reading a book three times quickly is overwhelmingly more effective in helping you to commit to memory what you've learned.
These are the things I've come to realize through experience.

26

Manage time.

Everyone is given time.

Inborn abilities don't vary that much from person to person.

If that's the case, don't you think victory or defeat in life hinges on how you manage your time?

Time is life itself.

To manage time is also to value life. If you waste another person's time, it's as reprehensible as shortening their life. When it comes to time, it doesn't hurt to think about it in such serious terms.

To spend time effectively, you need to carry out your work in the correct order of priority. In addition, you need to work efficiently by letting your daily routine sink into you. To put these two points into practice, I pored through every available business book and finally arrived at a certain approach. From that point on, the efficiency of my business improved by leaps and bounds. When I had my staff members try this, productivity rose instantly, and only a few of them continued to work overtime or on holidays.

This method is comprised of three administrative approaches, which I call The Three Sacred Treasures. They are as follows:

time management

task management

and what I call "knock management"

THE THREE SACRED TREASURES I

TIME MANAGEMENT

For most members of society, more than one-third of their day is spent on work, and they never seem to have any time to spare. To spend such busy days effectively, scheduling is essential. Previously, I used to make tight schedules, planning my days down to every last minute. But that only reduced my efficiency. I was preoccupied with time alone and my concentration had begun to wane considerably.

So I divided a single day into roughly four equal parts and decided to fill them with activity descriptions that were only approximate. Within each of these four time zones, I made it a point to not do anything whatsoever than the items I'd decided beforehand to carry out. Making my schedule approximate this way greatly improved my work organization and I became less prone to making mistakes.

In addition, I decided to regard one waking hour as one cycle of time, and made it a strict rule to take a ten-minute break after every 50-minutes of work. I urge you to try this approach. You should begin to actually feel that a single day is longer than you'd been imagining all along.

— 1 / 4

6:00 a.m. to 12:00 noon: input (information gathering)/the reason phase

On reporting to the office, I rigorously collect information on management and prominent individuals from newspapers, magazines, and books. Then I browse through five or six newspapers and 15 to 20 subscribed magazines. As for books, I read through 40 to 50 of them every month. An hour in the morning is worth two to three hours in the evening or at night. In my case, in order to concentrate, I don't answer the telephone, nor do I meet with people. I confine myself in my room and study.

— 2 / 4

12:00 to 6:00 p.m.: output (meetings and business discussions)/the sensitivity phase

To prepare for the coming afternoon, first of all I take a 15-minute nap on the futon I keep in the office. Then I proceed with meetings, business discussions and negotiations, or communicate with my subordinates. Since I'm not that sociable, I tend not to meet with people from outside very much. While many managers like to do this and engage in idle talk, I don't have much faith in business dealings that arise from such moments.

— 3 / 4

6:00 p.m. to midnight: private time (dining with others, engaging in pastimes) /the instinct phase

Free time. I go wild, using this time to dine with the staff or carry out some extra work. I leave the office at 9:30 p.m. and become absorbed in a pastime, such as studying areas that could possibly lead to businesses in the future. In any case, I take it easy and enjoy yoga and stretch exercises for 30 minutes before bedtime.

— 4 / 4

midnight to 6:00 a.m.: sleep/the rest phase

Incidentally, when I travel, if it's a long distance, I study, and if it's short, I indulge in people-watching. I observe with such concentration that I'll never forget even someone I've seen only once.

I work on Saturdays as well, and on Sundays I sort and review the information I've collected during the week. Following that, for about half a day, I do some shopping or entertain myself by watching movies, and so on. Since I rest well on weekdays, I don't feel any particular need to let my body rest on days off.

For my time management purposes, I don't use the type of personal organizers sold at stores, since they don't provide enough writing space. For my daily schedule, I create one on the PC and print it out on an A4-sized sheet of copying paper, and carry it along with me in a document folder that also contains an A4-sized notepad. On the following pages you'll find some sample pages from my customized personal organizer.

☐ Date

☐ Affirmation

I am energy. A crystallization of energy. A crystallization of energy that has the power to overcome anything. This is why I can never lose. Not even to illness or fate. Not to anything.

Today's schedule ※job...project name/hours...time required/action...description of task

06:00··· job | hours (:)
action

07:00··· job | hours (:)
action

08:00··· job | hours (:)
action

09:00··· job | hours (:)
action

10:00··· job | hours (:)
action

11:00··· job | hours (:)
action

12:00··· job | hours (:)
action

13:00··· job | hours (:)
action

14:00··· job | hours (:)
action

15:00··· job | hours (:)
action

16:00··· job | hours (:)
action

17:00··· job | hours (:)
action

18:00··· job | hours (:)
action

19:00··· job | hours (:)
action

20:00··· job | hours (:)
action

Review of yesterday

Start of work: ______ Actual work time ____ hours

End of work : ______ Break time ____ hours

Time spent on input ___ hours

Time spent on output ___ hours

Health condition __________

Today's results

※input...information acquired/output...information conveyed

06:00… job ______ hours (:)
input… output…

07:00… job ______ hours (:)
input… output…

08:00… job ______ hours (:)
input… output…

09:00… job ______ hours (:)
input… output…

10:00… job ______ hours (:)
input… output…

11:00… job ______ hours (:)
input… output…

12:00… job ______ hours (:)
input… output…

13:00… job ______ hours (:)
input… output…

14:00… job ______ hours (:)
input… output…

15:00… job ______ hours (:)
input… output…

16:00… job ______ hours (:)
input… output…

17:00… job ______ hours (:)
input… output…

18:00… job ______ hours (:)
input… output…

19:00… job ______ hours (:)
input… output…

20:00… job ______ hours (:)
input… output…

THE THREE SACRED TREASURES II

TASK MANAGEMENT

Prioritize your tasks and gain control over your life.

But it's really not that simple, is it? After all, most of your day tends to get filled up with unplanned tasks, like dealing with visitors who suddenly show up, answering unsolicited telephone calls, responding to work-related accidents or emergencies, attending formal occasions held by clients, rewriting documents, and encouraging colleagues.

If you were to deal with such goings-on in earnest all the time, you wouldn't have any meaningful time in the day left for yourself. This happens because unplanned tasks from here and there tend to keep arising unexpectedly, the more you keep trying to manage them.

So I recommend that you list up your daily tasks and categorize them into a total of four different types according to their degree of urgency and importance. This is what's known as task management, and if you keep doing it, you'll quickly be able to see your order of priority.

I make it a point to have a grasp of my employees' work situations by having them e-mail their task management lists to me. If I notice any error in their "order of priority," I make sure to advise them of it right away.

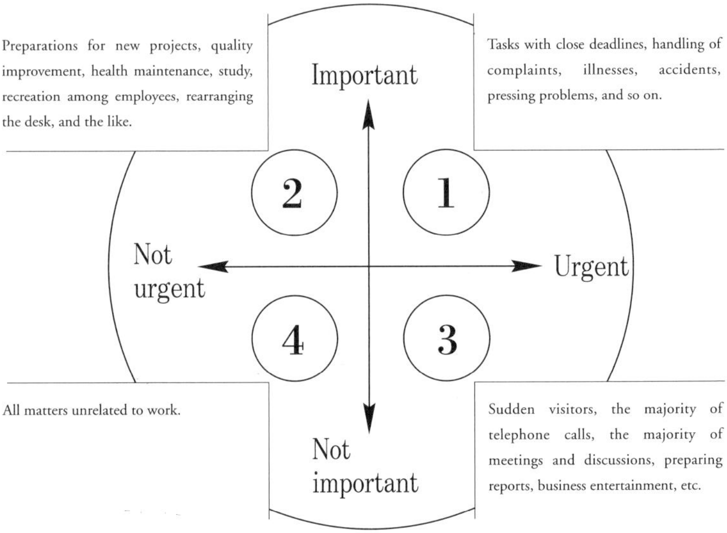

Needless to say, as much as possible you should start with matters that fall into Category No. 1 ("urgent and important") as soon as possible, and ignore those that fall into Category No. 4 ("not urgent and not important").

Keep a close eye on Category No. 2 ("not urgent but important"). Your level of work satisfaction will largely depend on how much time you allocate here, and this in turn will hinge on how much you reduce matters that fall into Category No. 3 ("urgent but not important").

The good news is that this is really easy. All you need to do is reduce useless phone calls, meetings, and social relationships. Even when it is necessary to be social with someone, just take the initiative and wrap up the conversation as early as possible.

Also, save as much time as possible at meetings. E-mail progress reports beforehand and reserve face-to-face meetings strictly for brainstorming sessions and resolving problems. This way, you should find that your time will become more productive, and as a result you'll be able to get around to working on the high-priority tasks.

Within a single day, many things come up that need to be done. When several tasks arise at the same time, many people fret over which one they should start with. But there's no need to worry, thanks to what's known as the "law of 2:8." This law states that if you concentrate on the really important 20 percent of your tasks, the remaining 80 percent will usually take care of themselves. So this means that if you can't finish everything immediately, concentrate on only 20 percent and put off the remainder until the next day.

If you keep on with this approach, you'll stay enthusiastic about your work for a long time. What's more, no matter how heavy your workload becomes, you won't find yourself getting physically or mentally exhausted.

THE THREE SACRED TREASURES III

KNOCK-MANAGEMENT

The word "knock" in "knock management" refers to the Japanese use of the word, which refers to fungoes (that is, fly balls) hit in baseball fielding practices. Just like practicing a thousand-fungo drill, brushing your teeth, or locking the doors to your house, you should be able to prepare for work or carry out routine jobs without much conscious effort. Doing so will help you become less absentminded and distracted, and more creative instead.

Toward this end, I would like you to create a checklist to help you in examining yourself. This checklist should show all those tasks that are obvious but are easy to forget, such as going through message memos, sending out thank-you letters to your work partners, carrying out task management, tidying up your desktop, and sorting through the business cards you've received.

	Tasks	1	2	3	4	5	6	7	8	9	10	11	12	13	14	15	16	17	18	19	2
	Write out daily report	○	○	○	○	○			○	○	○	○	×			○	○	○	○	×	
	Sort out tasks	○	○	○	○	○			○	○	○	○	○			○	○	○	○	○	
	Check Company A's website	○	○	○	○	○			○	○	○	○	○			○	○	○	○	○	
	Check Company B's website	○	○	○	○	○			○	○	○	○	○			○	○	○	○	○	
	Check Company C's website	○	○	○	○	○			○	○	○	○	○			○	○	○	○	○	
	Rearrange the desk	○	○	○	○	○			○	○	×	○	○			○	○	○	○	○	
	Sort out email	○	○	○	○	○			○	○	○	○	○			○	○	○	○	○	
	Sort through received business cards	○	○		○	○			○	○	○	○	○			○		○	○	○	
	Greet all employees	○	○	○	○	○			○	○	○	○	○			○	○	○	○	○	
	Go through message memos	○	○	○	○	○			○	○	○	○	○			○	○	○	○	○	
	Send out thank-you letters to clients	○	○	○	○	○			○	○	○	○	○			○	○	○	○	○	
	Work on reducing speech mannerisms like "well" & "um"															○	○	○	○	○	
	Clean bathroom	○	×	×	○	×	○	○	○	×	×	○	○	○	×	○	×	○	○	○	○
	Take out garbage	○		○		○			○		○		○			○		○		○	
	Water flowers	○	○	○	○	○	○	○	○	○	○	○	○	○	○	○	○	○	○	○	○
	Polish shoes	○	○	○	○	○			○	○	○	○	○			○	×	○	○	○	

Be sure to include not only work-related tasks but also private ones, such as cleaning the bathroom at home, polishing your shoes, and taking out the garbage. At the end of the day, mark completed tasks with a circle and the ones you goofed off on with a cross. In this way, you'll be able to objectively monitor yourself for the day and make any necessary adjustments to your routine.

For me, this is an important ritual that helps me to examine myself and firmly align my daily life with my major goals in life.

27

LIVE STRONG.

The legendary feudal ruler Oda Nobunaga desired a world that could be conquered through the sword, but I want to imagine a world that can be conquered through dreams. A world where people of different stripes, instead of fighting each other, pursue their own interests and achieve unity in the process. A world where one person's dream suddenly turns into everyone's dream, like a piece of fabric spreading out and covering everything under the sun.

Noblesse oblige is a concept that emerged from French chivalry and means that

with wealth, power, and prestige come social responsibilities of commensurate weight.

If you want to leave behind a life of mediocrity and lead a more rich and meaningful existence,

discover your ideal self, focus your energies on what stirs your soul, and keep sharing the everlasting wealth of your spirit.

BE BOLD.

Dreams don't come to you from somewhere else.

TAKE THE FIRST STEP NOW.

To die with passion.

Naoe Fumitada

Born in Taipei, Taiwan Province in 1977, Fumitada Naoe is the CEO of Sanctuary Corporation. He spent his early childhood in poverty, living in a shanty. Going on to move to Japan, he grew up feeling self-conscious about his Chinese-immigrant identity. Subsequently, the company run by his stepfather went bankrupt and his family dispersed. Though uncertain times ensued, he firmly resolved to become the world's No. 1 entrepreneur. When a childhood friend passed away in 2003, he began to harbor doubts about the existing state of the funeral business and went on to establish Sanctuary Corporation to pursue what a truly happy ceremony could be for the departed and the bereaved. By the age of just 27 he had managed to help the company grow into a business with an annual turnover of 3 billion yen.

Takashi Owaki

Born in 1971 in Aichi prefecture, Takashi Owaki is a photographer whose works have been exhibited in New York, Tokyo, and Kyoto, among other places. After studying construction at Mie University, he moved to the United States and majored in photography for one year at the International Center of Photography (I.C.P.), an institution established by Cornell Capa. He then went on to work as a cameraman's assistant in New York, while shooting his own works there for three years until the summer of 2002, when he returned to Japan. Today, he remains active in Tokyo and Nagoya, creating works that revolve around the themes of joy, life, and children.

Live with meaning. Die with passion.

Author **Fumitada Naoe**
Photography **Takashi Owaki**
Binding and design **Shimpachi Inoue**

Translated by **Raj Mahtani**
Arranged by **TranNet KK**

Published by **One Peace Books, inc. ,New York, New York**

One Peace Books, inc.
57 GREAT JONES STREET NEW YORK, NY10012 USA
TEL: 212-260-4400 FAX: 212-995-2969
URL : http://www.onepeacebooks.com

PRINTED IN JAPAN